James
REAL FAITH FOR THE REAL WORLD

Tim Stafford

ZondervanPublishingHouse
Grand Rapids, Michigan

A Division of HarperCollinsPublishers

MW00829945

James: Real Faith for the Real World
Copyright © 1995 by Tim Stafford

Requests for information should be addressed to:

📖 ZondervanPublishingHouse
Grand Rapids, Michigan 49530

ISBN: 0-310-49831-7

All Scripture quotations, unless otherwise indicated, are taken from the *Holy Bible: New International Version®*. NIV®. Copyright © 1973, 1978, 1984 by International Bible Society. Used by permission of Zondervan Publishing House. All rights reserved.

All rights reserved. No part of this publication may be reproduced, stored in a retrieval system, or transmitted in any form or by any means—electronic, mechanical, photocopy, recording, or any other—except for brief quotations in printed reviews, without the prior permission of the publisher.

Cover design by Jeff Sharpton, PAZ Design Group
Cover photograph © Carr Clifton
Interior design by Joe Vriend

Printed in the United States of America

97 98 99 00 01 02 / ❖ DP / 10 9 8 7 6 5 4

CONTENTS

GREAT BOOKS OF THE BIBLE

[E]very book of the Bible is important, because each one is inspired by God. But certain books draw us to them time and again for their strong encouragement, powerful teaching, and practical wisdom. The Great Books of the Bible Series brings into one collection eight biblical books that distinguish themselves either because of their undisputed excellence or because they are perennial favorites.

The Psalms, with their poetic imagery, help us express our emotions to God and see the myriad ways God works during the best and worst times of our lives. Two books—Proverbs in the Old Testament and James in the New Testament—offer practical wisdom for dealing with the decisions and realities of everyday life. The gospel of John gives us the most intimate and personal view of Jesus, the God-become-man who is Savior and Lord.

Three books are letters written by the apostle Paul. Romans is Paul's masterpiece—the clearest and fullest explanation of the gospel found in Scripture; there we see our world through God's eyes. Philippians shows us how to experience joy when we are under pressure. Ephesians explores the crucial role of the church as a living community, giving us just a little taste of heaven on earth as we seek to serve the Lord.

The series ends where the Bible does—with Revelation, the last book of the Bible, where we glimpse our glorious future, when all things will become new.

Whether you are a new student of God's Word or one who has studied these books many times before, you will find here new insights and fresh perspectives that will make the Bible come alive for you.

The Great Books of the Bible Series is designed to be flexible. You can use the guides in any order. You can use them individually or in a small group or Sunday school class. Some of the guides have six studies; others have as many as thirteen. Moreover, these books help us discover what the Bible says rather than simply telling us the answers. The questions encourage us to think and explore options rather than merely filling in the blanks with one-word answers.

Leader's notes are provided in the back of each guide. They show how to lead a group discussion, provide additional information on questions, and suggest ways to deal with problems that may come up in the discussion. With such helps, someone with little or no experience can lead an effective study.

Suggestions for Individual Study

1. Begin each study with prayer. Ask God to help you understand the passage and to apply it to your life.

2. A good modern translation, such as the *New International Version,* the *New American Standard Bible,* or the *New Revised Standard Version,* will give you the most help. Questions in this guide are based on the *New International Version.*

3. Read and reread the passage(s). You must know what the passage says before you can understand what it means and how it applies to you.

4. Write your answers in the spaces provided in the study guide. This will help you to express clearly your understanding of the passage.

5. Keep a Bible dictionary handy. Use it to look up unfamiliar words, names, or places.

Suggestions for Group Study

1. Come to the study prepared. Careful preparation will greatly enrich your time in group discussion.

2. Be willing to join in the discussion. The leader of the group will not be lecturing, but will encourage people to discuss what they have learned in the passage. Plan to share what God has taught you in your individual study.

3. Stick to the passage being studied. Base your answers on the verses being discussed rather than on outside authorities such as commentaries or your favorite author or speaker.

4. Try to be sensitive to the other members of the group. Listen attentively when they speak, and be affirming whenever you

6

can. This will encourage more hesitant members of the group to participate.

5. Be careful not to dominate the discussion. By all means participate! But allow others to have equal time.

6. If you are the discussion leader, you will find additional suggestions and helpful ideas in the leader's notes at the back of the guide.

Introduction

Real Faith for the Real World

I have a friend—I'll call her Sylvia—who has never grown up. It is not her fault. Sylvia began life with birth defects that arrested her development. Although she is now in her thirties, she behaves like a five-year-old.

Sylvia can be delightfully spontaneous. Often when I meet her, she greets me with a big smile and warm hug. She expresses enthusiasm and love freely. Like a child, she says exactly what she thinks. She also expresses irritation volubly; if something you do annoys her, you will know it instantly.

Sylvia's irritation carries no sting. Because Sylvia cannot help being what she is, her friends enjoy her as she is. We actually take pleasure in her impetuous, self-centered personality.

That makes Sylvia an exceptional person. Generally we don't want people to stay children. Childhood is a stage—a wonderful stage—but one to grow out of. It is sad when adults behave as though they have never grown up. And some do. The mere passage of years does not automatically turn people into authentic grown-ups.

Nor do years guarantee that Christians will become mature. Sometimes Christians who have been believers for a considerable time still act like children:

— They are very up and down—terribly enthusiastic about whatever engages them, completely bored with what doesn't.
— Like children, they can plunge headlong into a new activity, but they become impatient when it doesn't seem to bear results the way they expected.
— They consider suffering intolerable.
— They are interested in whatever affects them, not in what is valuable to others.

— They can be quick to judge those whom they regard as superficial or uncommitted or misguided.

— Their behavior often does not reflect the kind of faith they profess.

"Growing up" is James's subject. In practical, down-to-earth language this book describes Christian maturity and how to get there. James sets the attitudes that a grown-up Christian should have: perseverance, humility, and patience. Regarding the way we talk, our tendency to judge others, our response to wealth or suffering or sickness, James is plainspoken about Christian behavior. James teaches that it is not just what you believe that counts—it's your whole life.

The style of the book of James is radically different from that of letters like Romans or Philippians. The book jumps freely from subject to subject without trying to explain how they are connected. James, in fact, has been called "the Proverbs of the New Testament." Like the Old Testament book of Proverbs, the emphasis is practical. Also like Proverbs, the style is pithy and pictorial. James circles back to the same words and subjects repeatedly. The writing is like a mosaic: you have to step back in order to see the big picture.

The "big picture" is maturity. James does not want to leave young Christians at their natural level. The book aims to push them toward something better—toward grown-up behavior in Christ. As you study James, you will be challenged to grow into the kind of person Jesus wants you to be.

Perseverance

James 1:1–18

It begins as a sneaking suspicion when things don't go well. As troubles continue, a sense of doom or resignation can develop. "I must be doing it wrong," we think. "This is too hard. Surely God did not mean life to be such a struggle."

James takes a different point of view. Life is indeed a struggle, he writes, and for a good purpose. Through difficulties we learn perseverance, the art of "hanging in there." Christian growth, as James sees it, is a process for which there are no shortcuts. It takes time for God to teach us how to be mature people.

1. What was the hardest year of your life? How did that year affect your character?

2. Read James 1:1–18. In your own words, how would you define *maturity* (v. 4)?

3. What does James say is the role of trials in developing maturity?

4. If there are trials in your life that require special perseverance just now, what kind of maturity do you see potentially developing?

5. The Bible defines "wisdom" (v. 5) as skillful living—knowing how to conduct your life in a way that leads to good results. In what areas do you see people in our society showing a lack of wisdom? *media, parents, behavior priority. reaction instead of prayer. lack of responsibility*

6. What are the characteristics of a "double-minded" person (v. 8)? *conscencious trendy - lacks maturity lack not committed to anything therefor he can't grow in anything Doesn't must God.*

Why would such a person have trouble becoming wise and mature?
Crushed by the waves lack of maturity

Heb. 6 anchor of your 12 by- Johnson souls. Darwin on trial Book It couldn't just happen revelation

These are good questions because God has all the answers.

7. Verses 9–11 imply that trials of life erase superficial distinctions between the rich and the poor. Why would that be true?

How does the illustration of a wildflower make that point?

Rich - content with what you have.
poor -
poverty - of the Soul. Rich in mercy. *E. glay of God*

8. Verse 12 refers to the "crown of life" that God will someday give those who love him. What do you understand this "crown of life" to be, and how can anticipating it help us to persevere during trials? *hope*

crown of life those you live
for the love of Christ . Jam 1-12
Rev 2 10

9. Sometimes people put the blame on God for their failings. How does James describe the true origin of temptation (vv. 13–15)?

10. Some people regard temptation itself as sin, but the Bible indicates that is not the case. How do we keep from crossing the line from temptation to sin?

13

Do not relate the experience aloud to others, but try to think of an occasion when you did not cross the line, or another when you did. What were the results in your life? In others' lives?

11. If we know God as the changeless "Father of the heavenly lights" (v. 17), how will that knowledge of his character affect the way we deal with trials and temptations?

12. Verse 18 says that God intends Christians to be "a kind of firstfruits," which is the first crop a farmer harvests. What does this image add to your idea of maturity?

Memory Verse Every good and perfect gift is from above, coming down from the Father of the heavenly lights, who does not change like shifting shadows. He chose to give us birth through the word of truth, that we might be a kind of firstfruits of all he created.

—James 1:17–18

Between Studies

It is a good idea to "count your blessings," but we often apply that only in the most obvious sense. James encourages us to see God's blessing in periods of trial. During this week, draw up a list of various trials you have undergone in the course of your life. For each one, think about how you personally were affected. What aspects of your character were "completed" during that period?

Trials	Character developed
1.	
2.	
3.	
4.	
5.	

V. 2:13 Be merciful & forgive others
Only God in His mercy can forgive our
sin. We can earn forgiveness by
forgiving others - But when we with-
hold forgiveness we show we don't
understand or appreciate God's mercy toward us

LESSON 2
HEARING AND RESPONDING
JAMES 1:19 – 2:26

Modern life is overrun with stimuli. In the car we listen to music or news or talk shows. At home the TV is often on whether or not we really like the program. The telephone brings people into our lives whom we might otherwise seldom encounter. We hardly have a quiet moment.

Yet we are bombarded with so many stimuli that we also become adept at tuning things out. Most of us become good at hearing but not responding. We can't, after all, intensely feel with every crisis we hear on the news. We can't respond to every opportunity that is offered us.

The trouble begins when we apply the same distance to God. We hear his Word, but its urgency is lost on us. We don't answer. That, according to James, is a disastrous way to live.

1. How do we "turn off" various stimuli in modern life?

    turn off the T.V.
    Don't look at magazine, News papers
    Radio

2. Read 1:19–2:13. What practical responses does James say a Christian must take?

    to listen, slow to speak, slow to anger
    V.1-19 Don't anger when we are not heard or
    neglected or don't win an argument.
    (Selfish anger 17 never helps anybody)
    anger from a Bruised ego However when
    injustice + Sin occur we should become
    angery. plant the word in you, It will save
    you

What responses, practically speaking, must a Christian avoid? *to restrain from anger.*
or Avoid anger —

3. We have been taught that it is normal and natural to be angry and that we should express feelings openly regardless of the consequences. How do James's words on anger in verses 19–20 support or oppose this idea?

For a man's anger does not bring about the righteous life that God desires. anger = self-ego unless, it is righteous anger (injustice or sin when others are hurt.

others are hurt.
being

4. James does not condemn human anger, but he describes it as limited: it "does not bring about the righteous life God desires." According to verse 21, what *does* bring about this kind of life?

5. James makes clear that God has taken the initiative with the "word of truth" (v. 18). God is the one who "chose to give us birth" through it (v. 18), and "planted" it in us (v. 21). Describe how you see God doing this in your own life.

6. If a person listens to God's Word but doesn't act on it, what happens?

7. James devotes a long section (2:1–9) to the problem of favoring rich over poor in the church. If you see this as a problem today, explain. Why do you think this happens?

8. Twice in this section (1:25; 2:12) James refers to the "law that gives freedom." Laws are usually seen as restricting freedom. Why do you think James describes God's Word as giving freedom?

9. Read James 2:14–26. Why do you think James feels it necessary to emphasize that "faith without works is dead" (2:17, 26)?

10. How does James's assertion about works compare with Paul's assertion that we are saved by faith alone (Rom. 4:13)? How can both statements be true?

11. James backs up his argument that "faith without works is dead" by referring to the evidence of Abraham and Rahab. They represent two extremes of the family of faith: one was the famous father of Israel, and the other a foreign prostitute. What point is James making by referring to these two people?

12. What steps can we take personally to improve our "listening" in response to this passage?

Memory Verse
The man who looks intently into the perfect law that gives freedom, and continues to do this, not forgetting what he has heard, but doing it—he will be blessed in what he does.

—James 1:25

Between Studies

As noted in our study, Abraham was cited by the apostle Paul as an example of salvation by faith. James, making a related point, cites Abraham as an example of faith that results in action. This week, study the life of Abraham in Genesis 12–22. Make a list with three columns. In the first column, summarize each message that Abraham heard from God. In the second column, list the various actions Abraham took in response to God. In the third column, write down how his faith was involved in that response. (Note that not everything that God said to Abraham demanded action in response. Many of God's words were promises Abraham could only believe.)

God said, "Leave your country . . . " (Gen. 12:1).	Abraham left for a new land.	He trusted that God would provide for his needs.

Words That Hurt, Words That Heal

James 3:1–12

Speech, some say, is what distinguishes humans from animals. The ability to think and to communicate those thoughts to others sets humanity apart from all other creatures.

Words help us express our feelings and our ideas. They can build others up, encourage them, teach them. Or, words can wound, deceive, discourage.

James reminds us of the powerful way that words affect our relationships. More than that, James charts a link between the way we speak and the kind of people we become. Learning to control our tongues, James suggests, is a key to Christian maturity.

1. Think of a teacher who played a big role in your life. What made that person so helpful?

   Which had the greater impact—the material taught, or how it was communicated?

2. Read James 3:1–12. Verse 2 introduces the startling idea that a person with faultless speech will be fully mature. Based on your experience, how would you describe the link between the way a person talks and his or her character?

3. How do you think a person learns to say the right thing at all times?

4. Verses 3–4 compare our lives to horses and ships. What do they have in common?

5. What skills are required to keep a spirited horse under control with a bit?

Speech should be controlled by will & guided by wisdom & the word.

What skills are required to direct a ship with a rudder even in a strong wind?

Can you apply these same skills to directing your life through your speech?

6. If you would like to move your life in a more positive direction, what kinds of speech do you think are most likely to get you there?

    positive, kind, gental, Confendent God's wisdom uncouraging Praise & thanks giving yielding

    How can you adopt these positive kinds of speech into your everyday life?

7. Verses 5–8 use more negative imagery: a forest fire, an untamed animal, a deadly poison. Cite an experience or event when out-of-control talking was as destructive as these images imply.

8. In the same way that verse 2 asserts a connection between faultless speech and mature character, verse 6 connects the wrong kind of speech with a corrupt life "set on fire by hell." How can mere talk have this kind of impact on a person's life?

9. James says that very contradictory words come out of our mouths—especially our praise for God and our curses toward other human beings (vv. 9–12). What does this contradiction say about our inner lives, the source of our words?

10. What kinds of words could—or should—you eliminate from your life?

neg. don't, can't

11. James speaks of not only the potential destructiveness of ill-chosen words, but also the way that good words lead to maturity. If you were to become more thoughtful and skilled in your speech, in what ways could that affect your life?

Memory Verse

With the tongue we praise our Lord and Father, and with it we curse men, who have been made in God's likeness. Out of the same mouth come praise and cursing. My brothers, this should not be.

—James 3:9–10

Between Studies

This week take inventory on the way you talk. One approach is to focus on a particular relationship—with a spouse, a parent, a child, a neighbor or a co-worker—and take note of everything you talk about with that person in the course of three or four days. Keep a notebook with you, and write down the topic (and the actual words, where possible) of every exchange. When the time period is fulfilled, look over your records and evaluate the interaction. Were hurtful words said? Did your words encourage, instruct, admonish? How can you become a more effective conversationalist, more pleasing to God?

TWO KINDS OF SMART LIVING

JAMES 3:13 – 4:12

Sometimes Christianity is portrayed as a matter of acting in self-interest. The "health-and-wealth" gospel, which (in its crassest version) promises a Mercedes to those who ask God for it, portrays self-interest as a cardinal principle of faith.

James has a different version of the gospel. No doubt following God is good for people, but it follows a very different pathway from that of looking out for ourselves. The smart living of James's gospel involves humility before God. It means trusting him and putting others before ourselves.

1. Who is a role model for you? What makes his or her style of life admirable to you?

2. Read James 3:13–18. James contrasts two kinds of wisdom: one that is from heaven, and one that is from the devil. What are the characteristics of a person who has the devil's wisdom?

3. How can someone think of envy and selfish ambition as "wisdom?" Why would anybody boast about having these qualities?

4. Consider each of the characteristics of godly wisdom (3:17; see also 1:5–8). Describe an occasion when someone demonstrated godly wisdom.

   How can you cultivate these qualities?

5. James contrasts the results of earthbound wisdom with heavenly wisdom (vv. 15–18). Where in the world around you do you see those two kinds of results?

6. Read James 4:1–12. Verses 1–3 suggest that interpersonal quarrels stem from unsatisfied desires. Why, according to James, are our desires unsatisfied?

7. Why should you *not* pray so that you can "spend what you get on your pleasures" (v. 3)?

8. If you were to put the message of 4:4–5 into one sentence of modern English, what would you say?

9. These verses describe God as intensely envious, even though James 3:14–16 has just described envy as an aspect of worldly wisdom. When is jealousy appropriate?

10. Why is mourning a necessary part of submitting humbly to God (v. 9)?

11. James promises that if you humble yourself before God, "he will lift you up" (v. 10). What does it mean for God to lift us up? Why does it not mean that we will always get what we want (v. 2)?

12. In verses 11–12 James connects slandering other Christians with judging—condemning, or pronouncing judgment on—them. What attitude will a truly humble person have toward other Christians whom he sees acting questionably?

Memory Verse

The wisdom that comes from heaven is first of all pure; then peace-loving, considerate, submissive, full of mercy and good fruit, impartial and sincere.

—James 3:17

Between Studies

In Luke 6:32–35 Jesus says, "If you love those who love you, what credit is that to you? . . . But love your enemies, do good to them, and lend to them without expecting to get anything back. Then your reward will be great, and you will be sons of the Most High, because he is kind to the ungrateful and wicked."

The best way to turn from self-oriented worldly wisdom toward the humility of heavenly wisdom is to serve others who cannot repay you. This week, do at least one act of kindness for someone outside your ordinary circle: visit an elderly shut-in, for example, or help serve a meal at a soup kitchen.

<hr />

STUDY 5

PLANNING VERSUS PATIENCE

JAMES 4:13 – 5:20

The book of James begins with the radical affirmation that we should take joy in trials, because life's difficulties help us gain maturity. The book concludes by returning to some of the same themes.

What resources enable us to withstand trials? The self-sufficiency of the successful businessman or the wealthy landowner is mistaken, James says. In a second, one's assets can be wiped out. More profitable is a bank account full of patience and prayer, because we trust that God will triumph in the end.

But when will the end come? The Lord's coming is near, James affirms, yet Christ's return can seem to take a long time. In everyday life—which in biblical times as often as not meant farming—patience is essential. God's people have always shown patience, as we see in Scripture. Why, then, should patience be any less necessary today?

1. What makes you most impatient? Congested traffic? A long line at the grocery store? Meetings that go long? How do you act when you feel impatient?

2. Read James 4:13–17. On the surface it could appear that James is advising not to make plans. What is his concern?

3. Read James 5:1–12. From your experience, are rich people more likely to be self-confident, or humble? Why?

   Cite examples both of wealth being used for self-interest and of wealth being used for the benefit of others.

4. What is James's view of the personal security money can bring? How do people rich or poor seek security in money?

5. What do you think James would regard as the basis of real security?

6. James warns rich people not only because their money won't provide real security, but also because they have gained their wealth by cheating the poor. Where and how do you see James's warnings applying today?

7. Farmers, James says, provide a good example of patience. What enables a farmer to be patient?

8. James says "the Lord's coming is near," and "The Judge is standing at the door." Since these words were written nearly two thousand years ago, what should we understand them to mean?

9. From what you know of the Old Testament prophets, why would James point to them as examples of patience?

10. Why do you think James injects the issue of taking oaths into this discussion of patience?

11. Read James 5:13–20. How should a humble and patient Christian respond to unexpected circumstances?

12. James believes in the power of prayer. Experience shows, however, that not every sick person is healed. What do you think James would say about that?

Practically speaking, how do you think we should act on James's advice about prayers for the sick?

13. In view of verses 19–20, it is clear that Christians are mutually responsible to keep each other on the path to maturity. How can we help each other without being meddlers?

Memory Verse
Confess your sins to each other and pray for each other so that you may be healed. The prayer of a righteous man is powerful and effective.

—James 5:16

Between Studies

Elijah, whom James refers to as a model of effective prayer, spent his whole ministry contending with an unfaithful nation led by an idolatrous royal family. His success was limited, and his frustrations great. This week, study 1 Kings 16:29–19:18. Notice how often Elijah had to respond to unexpected events. Note also that he sometimes incorrectly evaluated a situation. What do you see sustaining Elijah in such times? Where do you see him modeling patience and trust in God? Where do you see impatience and mistrust?

LEADER'S NOTES

eading a Bible discussion—especially for the first time—can make
you feel both nervous and excited. If you are nervous, realize that
you are in good company. Many biblical leaders, such as Moses,
Joshua, and the apostle Paul, felt nervous and inadequate to lead others (see, for example, 1 Corinthians 2:3). Yet God's grace was suffi-
cient for them, just as it will be for you.

Some excitement is also natural. Your leadership is a gift to the
others in the group. Keep in mind, however, that other group members also share responsibility for the group. Your role is simply to
stimulate discussion by asking questions and encouraging people to
respond. The suggestions listed below can help you to be an effective
leader.

Preparing to Lead

1. Ask God to help you understand and apply the passage to your own life. Unless that happens, you will not be prepared to lead others.

2. Carefully work through each question in the study guide. Meditate and reflect on the passage as you formulate your answers.

3. Familiarize yourself with the leader's notes for the study. These will help you understand the purpose of the study and will provide valuable information about the questions in the study.

4. Pray for the various members of the group. Ask God to use these studies to make you better disciples of Jesus Christ.

5. Before the first meeting, make sure each person has a study guide. Encourage them to prepare beforehand for each study.

Leading the Study

1. Begin the study on time. If people realize that the study begins on schedule, they will work harder to arrive on time.

2. At the beginning of your first time together, explain that these studies are designed to be discussions, not lectures. Encourage everyone to participate, but realize that some may be hesitant to speak during the first few sessions.

3. Read the introductory paragraph at the beginning of the discussion. This will orient the group to the passage being studied.

4. Read the passage aloud. You may choose to do this yourself, or you might ask for volunteers.

5. The questions in the guide are designed to be used just as they are written. If you wish, you may simply read each one aloud to the group. Or you may prefer to express them in your own words. Unnecessary rewording of the questions, however, is not recommended.

6. Don't be afraid of silence. People in the group may need time to think before responding.

7. Avoid answering your own questions. If necessary, rephrase a question until it is clearly understood. Even an eager group will quickly become passive and silent if they think the leader will do most of the talking.

8. Encourage more than one answer to each question. Ask, "What do the rest of you think?" or "Anyone else?" until several people have had a chance to respond.

9. Try to be affirming whenever possible. Let people know you appreciate their insights into the passage.

10. Never reject an answer. If it is clearly wrong, ask, "Which verse led you to that conclusion?" Or let the group handle the problem by asking them what they think about the question.

11. Avoid going off on tangents. If people wander off course, gently bring them back to the passage being considered.

12. Conclude your time together with conversational prayer. Ask God to help you apply those things that you learned in the study.

13. End on time. This will be easier if you control the pace of the

discussion by not spending too much time on some questions or too little on others.

More suggestions and help are found in the book *Leading Bible Discussions* (InterVarsity Press). Reading it would be well worth your time.

Study One — *Perseverance*
James 1:1–18

Purpose To understand Christian growth as a process involving trials.

Question 1 Some people will not be emotionally ready to answer this question because "the hardest year of their life" entails very painful memories. If you are leading a group through this study, assure people that they can simply say, "I pass." For the rest, you will want to encourage people to keep their answers brief without going into detail. Otherwise the discussion may take up too much time.

Question 2 Maturity may seem like a very stodgy concept to some people, so it can be helpful to describe it in other words. James describes maturity as "complete, not lacking anything." A mature person has the spiritual and emotional wherewithal to respond to any and every kind of situation.

Question 5 Sexuality is one part of life that today seems particularly lacking in the application of wise living. People have strong feelings about their rights, but the end result of lax mores has been disastrous. AIDS, divorce, abortion, and promiscuity are some symptoms of our lack of wisdom.

Other areas can be mentioned: the treatment of the poor, care for God's creation, and the "marginalization" of religion in public life, for example.

Question 7 In the short run, a wealthy person and a wildflower are both attractive. Neither one, however, has staying power. If you watch long enough, you will see that their material riches are temporary.

James wants wealthy people to concentrate on areas of life where they do not "have it all together." It is in confronting their weakness and "low position" that they will move toward real maturity.

Question 8   The "crown of life" is the reward God will give to his followers at the end of history, when his kingdom is fulfilled. Some of Jesus' parables seem to suggest that this will involve holding actual authority over some realm. (See, for example, Luke 19:11–27.) Whatever one makes of this, it is clear that at the resurrection a Christian will be transformed, body and spirit (1 Corinthians 15:42–44, 50–55), and able to see and know God as never before (1 Corinthians 13:12).

Question 9   James says that temptations really begin in our desires. This is a very important point to note, because our modern era regards desire as quite neutral, if not prescriptive. The fact that someone has a persistent desire for sex or for a certain lifestyle or for others' admiration is regarded as proof that he *needs* what he wants. On the contrary, James says our desires can give birth to sin.

The result of sin, full-grown, is death. Death is the absence of life, and it has a spiritual as well as a physical meaning. Sin gradually moves us farther and farther from God to a place where we are spiritually as good as dead. Ultimately it will lead to the unrepentant sinner's destruction.

Question 10   We are sometimes made to feel guilty because we are tempted to sin. But Hebrews 4:15 clearly states that Jesus was tempted yet remained sinless. Thinking about this question can make us more aware of how to resist temptation.

Question 12   While maturity may sound fusty and unattractive, firstfruits are something longed for (through the whole growing season)—tasty and nourishing. Maturity may sound like something one wants only for oneself, but "firstfruits" are delightful and good for everybody.

Hearing and Responding

James1:19–2:26

Purpose   To understand that God works in our lives as we hear his Word and respond to it.

Question 1   For example: Throw away junk mail without looking at it. Mute the sound for television commercials. Hang up on telephone sales calls.

Question 2   Positively, James calls Christians to listen, to control their speech, to look after "orphans and widows," to feed and clothe those in need. Negatively, James urges Christians to avoid the pollution of the world, to restrain anger, to avoid favoritism for rich over poor.

Question 3   James does not deny that anger is normal, nor that it needs to be expressed. He does, however, urge caution about expressing anger hastily. James apparently recognizes that venting anger can cause damage. He also notes that, whatever expressing anger may accomplish for psychological health, it cannot achieve the goal of righteousness that God wants us to reach. In other words, while a person may need to express angry feelings, they can take him only so far. Real maturity goes beyond that.

Question 6   If you don't respond to God's Word, you simply forget it, and it makes no impact on your life. James's metaphor of the mirror can be compared to Jesus' parable of the sower (Luke 8:1–15). The seed on good soil "stands for those with a noble and good heart, who hear the word, retain it, and by persevering produce a crop." But unless seed sends roots down into deep soil, it cannot produce anything.

Question 7   Fascination with wealth is a classic symptom of "doublemindedness." Someone who favors rich over poor in church is trying to have it both ways: living by the world's value system while acting as though he or she is a disciple of Jesus. Such a divided mind can never gain much Christian maturity.

A church that favors rich over poor might have a desire to seem successful in others' eyes by attracting a wealthy congregation. They might also desire the financial contributions that a wealthy person can make. These are the kinds of desires that can be turned into sin.

Question 8   James wants to emphasize that Christ's law is a kind and generous master. It is for *our* sake that we are given the law: Obeying creates the kind of relationships that are really humane and livable, that free us to be the kind of people God meant us to be.

Question 10   Many readers through the centuries have understood James as contradicting Paul. Martin Luther regarded the book of James as an "epistle of straw" and questioned whether it is part of the canon of Scripture. It is not, however, necessary to understand Paul and James as being opposed.

James is correcting a tendency to misunderstand the gospel of grace. Some people, hearing of salvation by faith alone, understand faith as simply a mental assent. In reality, any genuine response to the gospel will result in a changed mind, which must result in changed actions. James is arguing that faith is a response of the whole person, not merely the intellect or the emotions. Paul would certainly agree.

Question 11   If in a group study there is time, you can refer to Abraham's sacrifice of Isaac in Genesis 22:1–19. Rahab's story is told in Joshua 2 and 6:22–23. It is worth noting that both Abraham and Rahab are cited in Hebrews 11, the "Faith Hall of Fame" (see vv. 17–19, 31).

Abraham and Rahab have very little in common except one crucial reality: God accepted them on the basis of their faith. (In Rahab's case, she was not even a Jew and did not follow the Old Testament law, yet God saved her and her family.) James's point is simply that they showed their faith in what they did—Abraham in his willingness to obey God to the extreme of sacrificing his son, Rahab in her risky protection of the Israelite spies. It is inconceivable that genuine faith should not result in action.

Study Three · Words That Hurt, Words That Heal

James 3:1–12

Purpose   To explore James's assertion that our lives are directed toward good or evil by the way we talk.

Question 4   Ships and horses are large and unwieldy and cannot be controlled by sheer strength or will power. Rather, they must be controlled by a very small mechanism: a bit or rudder. Similarly, our lives are not easily redirected; will power alone cannot change basic patterns. James is asserting that by controlling our tongues, we can move our lives in the direction we want to go.

Question 5   If you are in a study group, these questions may best be answered by those who are experienced riders or sailors. Some possible answers: close and constant attention to the reins or the rudder, anticipation of potential problems, experience that allows us to react instinctively to an unexpected situation.

Question 6   Some positive kinds of speech are thankfulness, encouragement, praise to God, truth-telling. They must be practiced daily if they are to become habitual.

Question 7   Many people can remember a thoughtlessly mean word that someone said to them as children. Often that word is festering still, many years later.

Gossip is also a source of considerable trouble in relationships. Friendships, families, and churches have all been torn apart by it.

Question 8   When careless talk becomes habitual, it destroys relationships. Meanness, selfishness, gossip, and flattery predominate. Friendships grow insincere and superficial. Living on such a deficient diet, a person can shrivel up emotionally and spiritually.

Question 9   If our words are impure and self-contradicting, our lives must be similarly impure and ambivalent. This is a basic problem in Christian maturity that James wants to address. He has previously mentioned the "double-minded" person (1:6–8) and the church that has a double standard for rich and poor (2:1–4).

Two Kinds of Smart Living

James 3:13–4:12

Purpose   To explore the difference between a life of self-oriented autonomy and a life of humble dependence on God.

Question 2   According to James, someone with the devil's wisdom harbors envy and selfish ambition, and this leads to disorder and evil deeds.

Question 3   The wisdom of a world without God is dominated by self. Its themes are "I do it my way" and "Take good care of yourself." Inevitably, it sees the self as competing with others, so that it is quite envious when someone else does well. This mindset seems sophisticated and wise, and people who live this way are often quite proud of their pragmatism.

Question 6   James offers two reasons why we have unsatisfied desires. The first is that we don't ask God. The implication is that we are too busy going after the things we want, trying to attain them through our own activities. This is the self-oriented "worldly wisdom" of 3:15–16.

The second reason for unsatisfied desires is that we ask God but with selfish motives. The problem is that we do not then approach God as God, but as a means to our ends. This is really just worldly wisdom under the guise of religiosity. We are praying, but not with the humility that James goes on to describe in 4:6–10.

Question 7   James uses strong language to address the question of our basic loyalties. Are we truly God's people? We can only be that in submission to him, for he is the Lord of the universe. But if we are ultimately loyal to our own worldly and selfish concerns, then we are "adulterous"—trying to act as though we are faithful to God while in reality craving another lover. When we pray so as to "spend what you get on our pleasures," we are in just that position. We are expecting God to serve us, rather than seeking to serve him.

Question 8   You may want to refer to Jesus' words in Matthew 6:24, where he warned that no one can serve two masters.

Question 9   God's envy echoes many Old Testament passages that proclaim God's jealous love for his people. There is only one God, and by his nature he cannot be in competition with anyone or anything else. If we put him into that kind of competition, we are in effect denying him and his claims on our lives. He is appropriately jealous for the love of his people. The most parallel situation is between husband and wife, where there is an appropriate kind of jealousy when one partner is unfaithful to the other.

Question 10 If we come before God as God, rather than as simply a source of the pleasures we seek for ourselves, his holiness and purity will make us deeply aware of our sinfulness and selfishness. We will need to change our self-confident laughter to repentant mourning.

Question 11 When God lifts us up, he does it by transforming us. Joy and satisfaction often come in a way that we never expected or wanted. For example, we may find ourselves very happy serving in a very humble capacity.

Study Five   *Planning Versus Patience*
James 4:13–5:20

Purpose To focus attention on the patient attitude that characterizes a mature Christian.

Question 2 James is not against planning *per se,* but rather, planning without humbly recognizing God's ultimate direction of our lives. Our future is always uncertain, subject to circumstances beyond our control. Only the Lord knows what will happen; he holds all circumstances in his hands. A mature Christian will not be overconfident in his plans, but will recognize his dependence on God.

Question 7 A farmer knows that his crops have a growing season that cannot be hurried. He is patient, working through the long months in which he reaps nothing, because he knows that harvest time is coming. Patience, James is saying, comes from our hope that the world is working toward its purpose, which will surely come because it is in God's hands.

Question 8 It may be that James and other New Testament writers expected Christ's return in their own time, but that is not the burden of their writing about the Second Coming. James does not even try to give an approximate date for Christ's return; he tries to prescribe the proper attitude Christians should have toward the contingency of the world we live in. The nearness of Christ's coming may be understood as being parallel to God's standing at the door—that is, Christ could come any moment; he is ready and waiting to return. We should live in such a way that we are always ready to see him, rather than thinking that we have plenty of time to put our lives in order.

In another sense, the Judge stands at the door of all our lives, for we do not know when we will die.

Question 9 Throughout the Old Testament, God's prophets proclaimed the truth about God and called his people to respond. With few exceptions, they were ignored. Many of them were persecuted for their truth-telling. Despite little encouragement, they continued to obey God and speak the truth. James is undoubtedly thinking of the thousands of years during which the prophets waited for God's promised Messiah. They were patient in sticking to the truth, not compromising their faith, trusting that God's plan would triumph.

Question 10 James is recalling Jesus' words in Matthew 5:33–37. The person who takes an oath is usually promising in the strongest way possible that he or she will fulfill an obligation. But as James has pointed out, nobody knows what will happen tomorrow (4:14). Rather than acting as though we are in charge of the future, we should speak simply and humbly, recognizing that God is the only one ultimately able to take oaths about the future. That is an attitude that engenders patience.

Question 12 The church has traditionally understood James's promise of healing in the sense of the complete salvation, body and spirit, that will come to every Christian in the fullness of the kingdom of God. Many diseases are healed here and now by prayer, but some will only be finally healed in the resurrection. Since in this chapter James has also been writing about waiting patiently for Jesus' return, it is not difficult to think that his utter confidence in prayer has this final healing in mind.

647-7808

graig
jickil